ABC

A B C D E F G
H I J K L M N
O P Q R S T U
V W X Y Z

ALPHABET

Alphabet Learning Picture Book For Kids Aged 2-5 Years

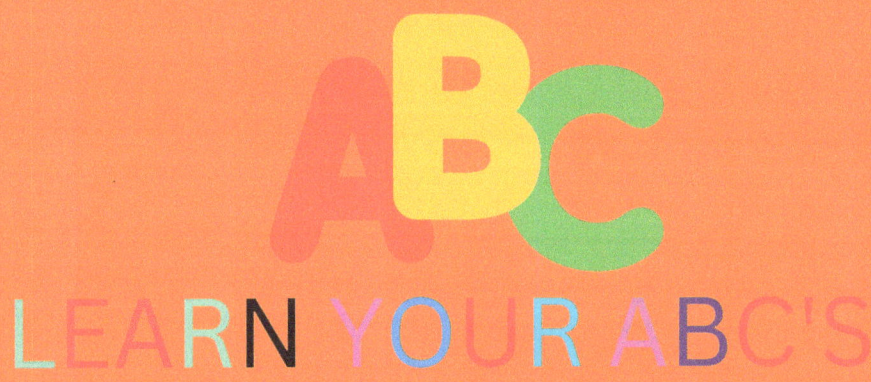

Educational children's book that takes young readers on a journey through the alphabet.

ISBN:978-1-916554-04-7

Apple

Bee

C

Caterpillar

d

Duck

e

Elephant

Frog

 Giraffe

Hippo

 Igloo

 Jellyfish

K Koala

l

Lion

Monkey

Newt

 Octopus

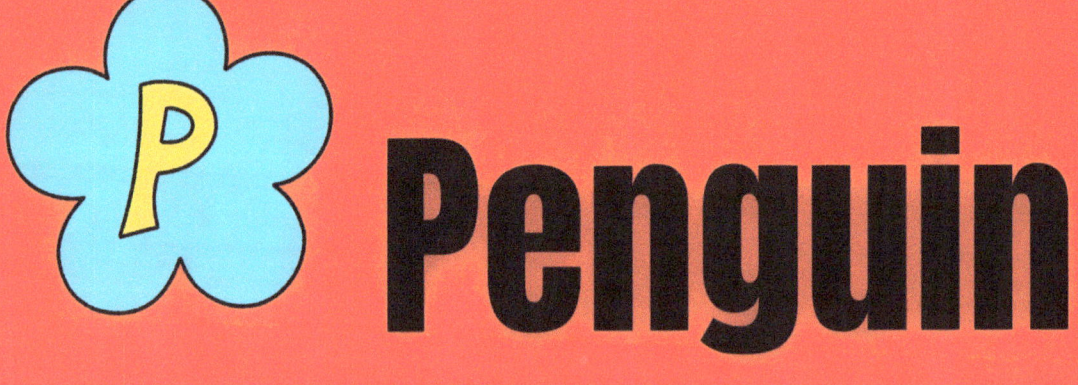
Penguin

 **Quail**

 **Rabbit**

 Squirrel

 # Violin

 Whale

Xylophone

Yoyo

 Zebra

www.ingramcontent.com/pod-product-compliance
Lightning Source LLC
Chambersburg PA
CBHW051322110526
44590CB00031B/4444